THE
HERO'S
PENALTY

Devin Carroll

THE
HERO'S
PENALTY

How **Social Security** Works
for **Educators**

DEDICATION

To my wife, Karen, for being a
partner in every sense of the word.

DISCLAIMER

This book is meant to be for educational and general information purposes only.

It does not provide specific tax, legal, or financial advice. Please consult with your own advisors for personalized advice around your specific situation.

This book, the author, or any of the related entities are not affiliated with or endorsed by the Social Security Administration or the US Government.

Acknowledgements

This book would still be a collection of words stuck in a computer if not for the help of many people.

Thanks to my wife, Karen, for encouraging me to set a deadline and get finished.

Thanks to my development team for making me look and sound polished: Kali Roberge for your wordsmithing and patient editing; Teddi Black for your patience in designing my cover art; and Megan McCullough for your ability to take a messed-up document lay it out into a well-designed book.

And as always… a big thank you to the readers of my blog, SocialSecurityIntelligence.com for being such great fans.

Table of Contents

Introduction

She was literally in tears.

My client worked as an educator for 32 years. Six months before she was scheduled to retire, her husband was killed in a tragic accident. Not only did she have to deal with the loss of her partner, but now, the Social Security Administration told her she would never collect a penny of her survivor's benefits -- all because she'd chosen to work in education.

She was a meticulous planner, and this was income that she and her financial planner counted on when building out her retirement income plan. That plan now had a big hole in it.

As my client sat in my office that day, she reflected on some of the decisions she'd made throughout her career. She told me she'd once been offered a job as a staff accountant. She nearly took that job, but ultimately decided to continue teaching. And then there was the time when she almost left teaching to stay at home with her kids.

She knew the teaching pay wasn't as good as the accounting job, and becoming a stay at home parent would have provided her with a lot of value and wonderful experience -- but she really enjoyed teaching. She felt passionately about it. Plus, she knew that every year she taught added a bit more to the pension she could eventually use as retirement income.

I still remember the look on her face when she said, "If I would have stayed at home instead of teaching, I would be able to get my full survivors benefit."

This is just one example of how strange some of the systems in our society really are. The majority of teachers are qualified to work jobs where their earnings could be higher (and in some cases, much higher). Instead, like my client, educators choose to work in the positions they feel offer more meaning and serve an important role for our kids -- and in jobs where they're also covered by a state pension instead of Social Security.

The result is a set of complicated rules that, ultimately, penalize our educators and teachers. I wish the story of my client who lost her husband, depended on the survivors benefits from Social Security, and could not receive them, was an isolated case. It's not.

Since that day I've talked to thousands of educators who have worked in a job where they did not pay Social Security tax and instead got a teacher's pension. Many of these educators started their careers when retirement seemed like it was so far away it would never come. But now that retirement was upon them, and only then did they find out horrible truth about their lack of benefits.

As I dug into it more, I realized that the average Social Security representative knew very little about the rules that prevented educators from receiving benefits. That added to the misinformation around and confusion on how to apply these rules.

The fact that Social Security coverage varies among states and sometimes even among school districts within the same state doesn't help, either. Currently, most teachers in Alaska, California, Colorado, Connecticut, Georgia, Illinois, Kentucky, Louisiana, Maine, Massachusetts, Missouri, Nevada, Ohio, Rhode Island, Texas, and the District of Columbia do not have coverage through Social Security.

But even within those states, there are pockets of participation. Texas, for example, has more than 20 school districts that participate in Social Security -- but the rest of the state's public schools do not. When educators move around between school districts that do participate and those that do not, it gets even more complicated.

Here's what all this means for you: the burden is on *you* to figure out Social Security, the benefits you can claim, and the best filing strategies to get those benefits.

Reading this book is an excellent first step in getting informed. I'm glad you've picked it up and have read it this far. There have been many in your situation who have prefered to believe that the topic is simply too complex to learn and apply. That is not the case! In this book, we'll break it down into digestible chapters that make the individual topics understandable.

But it's important to know: this book does not provide a deep dive into *all* of the nuances and exceptions that apply when working with public servant pensions and Social Security. It's intended to be an informative view that doesn't get bogged

down in every last precious detail. Why? Because I want you
to be able to get main concepts and understand them well
enough that you feel empowered to take action (and not left
feeling even *more* confused).

How to Read This Book

I've broken this book down into two separate parts. Before
you can fully understand the provisions that are applicable
to public servants, it's imperative that you have a firm grasp
on the basics of Social Security. You'll find that the rules
you face are built upon the basics. For example, if you don't
have a good grasp of spousal benefits, it will be difficult to
understand how the Windfall Elimination Provision reduces
those spousal benefits. The same can be said for many of the
foundational elements of social security and how they relate
to these rules.

For this reason, you'll want to consume this book in two
parts:

- **Part 1** covers the basics that will give you the
  knowledge you need to fully understand the
  complexities that apply to your specific situation.
  This is the foundation that the other rules are built
  upon. (If you read the first part of this book and find
  that you want more details on the fundamentals, then
  you might want to read my first book, *Social Security
  Basics*.)

- **Part 2** covers all the specifics of the rules that are
  specific to individuals, like teachers and professionals

working in education, who worked at a job where they did not pay Social Security taxes.

Read Part I carefully, and move forward *only* when you feel that you fully understand the basic concepts. Read it twice or even three times if that's what it takes to put you in a position where you feel comfortable with the fundamentals of how Social Security works -- otherwise, Part II will not make as much sense.

Ready to begin on those basics? Then let's dive in!

PART I

THE BASICS

Chapter 1

Social Security Credits and Your Earnings Record

Social Security credits are the building blocks that the Social Security Administration relies on to determine whether you qualify for one of its programs. In 2018, you receive one credit for each $1,320 of earnings, up to the maximum of four credits per year. The amount of earnings needed to earn a credit increases annually as average wage levels increase.

In exchange for the tax you pay, you earn eligibility for the following important benefits:

- Social Security Retirement Benefits

- Social Security Disability Benefits

- Social Security survivors benefits

How Credits for Each Program Work

Each of these programs have different requirements for the number of credits to gain eligibility:

Credits for Retirement Benefits

The Social Security credits required for retirement benefits are the easiest to understand. If you were born after 1929, you must be "fully insured" for eligibility. This simply means that you have earned 40 credits. In most cases, all 40 credits can be satisfied by 10 years of work. If you do not have enough Social Security credits based on your work history, you may qualify for a benefit on a spouse's work record.

Credits for survivors benefits

Social Security survivors benefits do not always require you to be fully insured (or to have 40 credits). An individual who does not have 40 credits may still be eligible for survivors benefits if they are "currently insured." The Social Security Administration defines "currently insured" as having at least six Social Security credits during the full 13-quarter period ending with the calendar quarter in which the worker dies. This means that if you haven't yet worked for 10 years, your survivors may still be eligible for benefits if you have worked at least 1.5 years of the prior 3.25 years.

Credits for Disability Benefits

Generally, the number of Social Security credits required for disability benefits is 40. You must also have recent work history. In fact, 20 of your credits must have been earned in the last 10 years ending with the year you become disabled (unless you're blind). Simply put, this means that you need to have worked in 5 of the past 10 years. Since disabilities can also happen to younger workers, there are some exceptions to the 40-credit rule.

Understanding Your Earnings Record

The amount of Social Security benefits one receives is a result of a formula which uses your earnings while you are working. These earnings are reported to the Social Security Administration on an annual basis. Well…they are supposed to get reported. It doesn't always happen. Mistakes in an individual's Social Security earnings record are actually much more common than most people think. In tax year 2012 alone, the Social Security Administration reported $71 billion in wages that could not be matched to an individual's earnings record.[1] The good news is that the Social Security Administration has an internal process for sorting out some of these mistakes and assigning the earnings to the correct record.

Even so, nearly half of the mismatches are never corrected. That means that in 2012 there were approximately $35 billion in wages that was never credited to an individual's Social Security history. On an annual basis, print your Social Security statement and verify that the earnings amounts are correct. You can print yours from your mySSA account at www.SSA.gov/myaccount.

Why is this such a big deal? Because a mistake in your earnings history can make a big difference in how your Social Security benefits are calculated. It all goes back to the benefits formula. We won't go into the full formula in this book, but as a summary, you should know that the Social Security Administration uses your highest 35 years of earnings as a cornerstone of the benefit calculation.[2]

---

1   https://www.ssa.gov/budget/FY16Files/2016OIG.pdf
2   https://www.ssa.gov/pubs/EN-05-10070.pdf

If any of these 35 years are incorrect or missing altogether, the average is skewed. One year of missing earnings can make a difference of $100 per month (or more!) in your benefit amount. Over your lifetime, that could be nearly $30,000 in missed benefits from one year of missing earnings.

Another very important consideration is the exemption you can get from the Windfall Elimination Provision if you have enough "substantial earnings" in your history. We'll get much deeper into the WEP in Part II of this book -- but for now, know that one missing year of earnings will completely change the formula that is used to calculate your benefit.

If you find a mistake in your earnings record, you want to get it corrected quickly. You'll need the following documents to get this done.

- REQUEST FOR CORRECTION OF EARNINGS RECORD (SSA Form 7008)

- Tax returns, pay stubs or other information from employer.

Call or visit your local SSA office and they'll tell you where to send the documents.

CHAPTER TAKEAWAYS

- You can earn up to 4 credits per year.

- The credit requirements for various programs are not all the same.

- You should check your earnings record annually

Chapter 2

Your Full Retirement Age

Your full retirement age is the age at which you can begin receiving benefits and receive 100% of your primary insurance amount (PIA), or your full retirement age benefit. Your full retirement age depends on the year of your birth.

For those born between 1943 and 1954, the full retirement age is 66 years old. If you were born between 1955 and 1960, your full retirement age will be age 66 plus 2 months for every year after 1954. Born in 1960 or later? Your full retirement age is 67.

BIRTH YEAR	FULL RETIREMENT AGE
1943-1954	66
1955	66 + 2 months
1956	66 + 4 months
1957	66 + 6 months
1958	66 + 8 months
1959	66 + 10 months
1960 & later	67

If you file at your full retirement age, you get full retirement benefits. But you don't have to file on this date. In fact, you can file earlier or later -- but there are some serious consequences to doing so. Here's what you need to know.

How Your Filing Age Increases or Reduces Your Benefit

If you file at an age other than your full retirement age, your benefit amount will be reduced or increased. Filing earlier than your full retirement age leaves you with a reduced benefit. Filing later, on the other hand, gives you an increased benefit. When you only need to calculate your benefit (not spousal or survivors benefits), the increases and decreases are pretty simple to understand.

Let's examine the increase first. If you wait to file, you'll receive a credit of 8% for every year you delay up until age 70. The Social Security Administration refers to these increases as "delayed retirement credits."

Social Security Benefit by Filing Age	
62	70%
63	75%
64	80%
65	86%
66	93%
67	100%
68	108%
69	116%
70	124%

Chart Assumes Age 67 Is Full Retirement Age

You only get the increase if you file late. If you file early, your full retirement age benefit actually drops below what you'd receive at full retirement age. How much your benefit is reduced depends on your age when you file. If you file at 66, just one year early, your benefit will be reduced by almost 7%. If you begin receiving benefits at age 62, your benefit would drop far more dramatically and be 30% lower than what you would receive at your full retirement age.

CHAPTER TAKEAWAYS

- Full Retirement age is not the same for everyone.

- Your benefits will be reduced or increased based on your filing age.

- The increases and reductions occur on a monthly basis.

Chapter 3
The Earnings Limit

At one of my first speaking engagements, an attendee shared this story with me: A few years before, she'd been at her bridge club when the topic turned to Social Security. As they chatted about it, the consensus around the table seemed to be that filing at 62 was the smartest thing to do. This lady, trusting the advice of some of her closest friends, filed for benefits as soon as she turned 62.

She then told me that she'd always wanted to buy a brand-new Toyota Camry. She figured that once she started receiving Social Security income, it would be the perfect time to buy the car. She was still working, which meant her Social Security check would be extra income. So that's exactly what she did: she bought the car, and took out a car loan that she planned to pay with the income from her Social Security benefits.

A few months later, she received a nasty letter from the Social Security Administration stating that she had been paid benefits that she was not eligible for. They asked her to pay the benefits back and informed her that her benefits would be suspended due to her income. Now she had a new car and a car loan, without the Social Security benefits to pay for it.

What happened here? Something that surprises more than just the poor Camry owner who approached me that day: The Social Security earnings limit.

Understanding the Social Security Earnings Limit

The Social Security earnings limit is the amount of money you can earn before that income from your work impacts your Social Security benefit. If your income exceeds the Social Security income limit (which is defined based on your specific situation), your Social Security benefits will be reduced proportionally. It's important to note that the earnings limit does not apply if you file for benefits at your full retirement age or beyond.

2018 Social Security Income Limits		
AGE	INCOME	CONSIDERATIONS
Under Full Retirement Age	$17,040	For every $2 over the limit, $1 is withheld from benefits
In the calendar year Full Retirement Age is reached	$45,360	For every $3 over the limit, $1 is withheld from benefits until the month of Full Retirement Age
At Full Retirement Age or older	No limit	None

These limits only apply to those who begin taking Social Security before reaching full retirement age. Specifically, the income limit depends on where you are in the Social Security timeline and your age:

The Time Between Receiving Benefits and Reaching Full Retirement Age

For each full calendar year between the year you begin receiving Social Security benefits and the year that you will reach full retirement age, you may earn up to $17,040 before your benefits are reduced.

The Year You Reach Full Retirement Age

In the year that you will reach full retirement age, the income limit increases to $45,360 (for 2018) without a reduction in benefits. This means that if you have a birthday in July, you'll have 6 months of an increased income limit before it drops completely off at your full retirement age. This increased limit allows many individuals to retire at the beginning of the calendar year in which they attain full retirement age.

After Full Retirement Age

Once you reach full retirement age, there is no reduction in benefits regardless of your income level.

Dealing with Reductions in From the Earnings Limit

There are two levels of benefits reduction. Like the income limit, benefit reductions are tied to your age (relative to your full retirement age).

For each year before the calendar year in which you reach full retirement age, you will lose $1 in benefits for every $2 that you earn beyond the Social Security income limit. In the year you will reach full retirement age, but before the month of your actual birthday, you will lose $1 in benefits for every $3 that you earn beyond the Social Security income limit.

What Kind of Income Counts as Earnings?

The Social Security income limit applies only to gross wages and net earnings from self-employment. All other income is exempt, including pensions, interest, annuities, IRA distributions and capital gains. The term "wages" refers to your gross wages. This is the money that you earn before any deductions, including taxes, retirement contributions, or other deductions.

WHAT COUNTS AS EARNINGS FOR THE SOCIAL SECURITY EARNINGS LIMIT?

WHAT DOES COUNT	WHAT DOES NOT COUNT
Employment Income	Pension Payments
Net Earnings from Self Employment	Annuity Payments
	IRA Distributions
	Dividends
	Interest Income
	Capital Gains

CHAPTER TAKEAWAYS

- If you are under full retirement age, there is a limit to the amount you can earn and draw Social Security.

- The earnings limit changes in the year you attain full retirement age.

- There is no income limit once you attain full retirement age.

- Not all income sources count against the income limit.

Chapter 4

Length of Marriage Rules and Spousal Benefits

If you've had prior marriages, it is crucial to know about length of marriage rules. The Social Security Administration has separate length of marriage rules for:

- Survivors benefits

- Spousal Benefits

- Divorced Spouses

The benefit that has the shortest length of marriage requirement is the survivors benefit. It only requires that you were married for nine months before you can file to receive it. There are a few reasons that this rule is waived for surviving spouses.

Broadly speaking, it could be waived if: (a) You are the natural or adoptive parent of the deceased worker's biological child, or (b) if the death was a result of accident. If one of these exceptions apply to you, the nine month marriage requirement does not apply.

Survivor Benefit - *9 Months*
Spouse Benefits - *1 Year*
Divorce Spouse - *10 Years*

Spousal benefits are easier to understand. The marriage must have lasted for one continuous year. Simple. The length of marriage requirement for divorced spouses, on the other hand, is 10 years.

The "divorced spouse" category is a little unique in that it is not a category on its own. As a divorced spouse, you may be entitled to either survivors benefits or spousal benefits. The determining factor as to which one you would be eligible for is the status of your ex-spouse. If they are alive, you could be eligible for spousal benefits. If they are deceased, you could be eligible for survivors benefits.

If you remarry prior to age 60, you lose the right to claim on an ex-spouse's record — at least until the subsequent marriages end in death or divorce. If you remarry after age 60, you're eligible to receive benefits based on whatever is highest: your benefit, a spousal benefit on your current spouse's, or your deceased spouse's survivors benefit. In the case multiple marriages, if all marriages have ended and you've met the length of marriage rules, you can choose the highest benefit from any of your ex-spouses.

How Spousal Benefits Work

The original Social Security Act provided retirement benefits only to the worker. Spouses were not eligible. In 1939, the law was amended to allow women to collect a spousal benefit. In 1950, men became able to draw a spousal benefit. Since, then the spousal benefit has become a very important part of retirement income.

If you're eligible and can qualify, the spousal benefit can be as much as 50% of the higher-earning spouse's full retirement age benefit. If your spouse's full retirement age benefit amounts to $2,000 per month, your spousal benefit at your full retirement age could amount to $1,000 per month.

This benefit cannot be more than 50% of the higher-earning spouse's full retirement benefit... but it can be less! The spousal benefit is also based on your filing age. Depending on how old you are when you file, the spousal benefit amount will range between 32.5% and 50% of the higher-earning spouse's full retirement benefit.

Check out the chart below to get an idea of how the benefit works and what your payment might be if you can take advantage of spousal benefits. The chart assumes that your full retirement age is 67 and your spouse's full retirement age benefit is $2,000 per month.

Your Spouse's Full Retirement Age Benefit Amount	Your Age	% of Your Spouse's FRA Benefit You Will Receive	Your Benefit Amount
$2,000	62	32.50%	$650
$2,000	63	35%	$700
$2,000	64	37.50%	$750
$2,000	65	41.66%	$833
$2,000	66	45.83%	$917
$2,000	67	50%	$1,000

Based on Full Retirement Age at 67.

CHAPTER TAKEAWAYS:

- There are different length of marriage rules for different benefit types.

- Spousal benefits are up to 50% of the higher earnings spouse's benefit.

- The higher earning spouse must file first before spousal benefits can be paid.

- When filing at separate times and ages the spousal benefit can be complicated.

Chapter 5

What to Know About Survivors Benefits

Social Security survivors benefits might be the one thing about Social Security that I can give a simple answer to: at death of the first spouse, surviving spouses are eligible to receive the higher of:

- Their own monthly benefit, or

- The monthly benefit of the deceased.

That's the clean and straightforward answer -- but of course, it's not quite that simple in real life. Every family is different. Unique situations and variables can introduce some complexity. Here's all the other information you need to know to better understand how survivors benefits work, starting with the fact that Social Security pays out two types of benefits upon death. The first is a lump sum death benefit. The second is the monthly survivors benefit.

The Lump Sum Death Benefit

Upon the death of a Social Security beneficiary, the Social Security Administration pays a lump-sum death payment of $255. Obviously, a one-time $255 payment doesn't quite cover the cost of a funeral. It's been stuck at that level for several years and inflation has significantly eroded its useful value, so it is no longer called the funeral benefit. It's now officially referred to as the lump sum death benefit.

There are three categories of people who may receive a lump sum death benefit from Social Security:

1. A surviving spouse, who was residing with the deceased spouse, or

2. A surviving spouse, who was not residing with the deceased, but was receiving benefits based upon the work record of the deceased spouse, or who becomes eligible for benefits after the death of the spouse, or

3. A surviving child, who was receiving benefits based upon the work records of the deceased parent, or who becomes eligible for benefit after the death of the parent. The payment is divided evenly among all eligible children.

If the eligible spouse or child is not receiving benefits at the time of death, they may receive the benefit if they apply for apply for benefits within two years of the death. If there are no eligible survivors in either of these three categories, then the SSA does not pay a lump sum death benefit.

Calculating Your Benefit Amount

Figuring out how much you'll receive in Social Security survivors benefits requires a little math. The simple explanation is that at the death of the first spouse, surviving spouses receives the higher of their own benefit, or the benefit of the deceased. But this simple explanation doesn't consider (a) what age the deceased filed for benefits, if they did at all, and (b) when the surviving spouse decides to file.

If the Deceased Did Not File for Benefits

If the deceased spouse never filed for benefits, but died on or before their full retirement age, the calculation is relatively easy. The survivor receives the deceased's full retirement age benefit, adjusted for the survivor's filing age.

If the deceased spouse never filed for benefits, and died after their full retirement age, the survivor receives the deceased's benefit in the same amount it would have been on the date of the deceased's death (including delayed retirement credits) reduced for the filing age of the survivor. But what if the deceased spouse filed for benefits before he passed away? If this is the case, it could get a little more confusing.

If the Deceased *Did* File for Benefits

If the deceased spouse filed for benefit on or after their full retirement age, and the surviving spouse is at full retirement age, the benefit amount payable to the survivor will remain unchanged. If the surviving spouse is less than full retirement age, the amount the deceased spouse was receiving would be reduced by the filing age of the survivor.

If the deceased filed for benefits before their full retirement age, the surviving spouse is entitled to the full retirement age benefit of the deceased (reduced for survivor's filing age) but will always be limited to the larger of the actual benefit of the deceased or 82.5% of the deceased's full retirement age benefit.

This 82.5% limit is a special rule often called the "Widow's Limit" but the technical name is the Retirement Insurance Benefit – Limitation (mostly referred to as the RIB-LIM.) It's meant to offer some protection for surviving spouses when the deceased spouse filed at, or near, the earliest age possible. This rule states that if your deceased spouse filed early, you'll be forever limited to either the amount they were drawing, or 82.5% of their full retirement age benefit. This rule has been a real lifesaver for some widows and widowers.

FILING AGE	% of DECEASED'S BENEFIT
60	71.50%
61	75.58%
62	79.65%
63	83.72%
64	87.79%
65	91.86%
66	95.93%
67	100%
68	100%
69	100%
70	100%

Based on Full Retirement Age at 67.

Advanced Filing Strategies for Survivors

In early 2018 the Office of the Inspector General released a report with some shocking news. 82% of widows and widowers who are receiving Social Security survivors benefits are actually entitled to a higher monthly benefit payment.[3] The only problem is, the Social Security Administration never made them aware of this. This affected an estimated 9,224 widows and widowers 70 and older who could have received an additional $131.8 million in Social Security benefits.

This is because the widow(er)s were never told that they could still use the filing strategies that were now off limits for everyone else. This guide does not have the space to cover these strategies, but I'd encourage you to read my free article Social Security survivors benefits: The Complete Guide. You can find that at socialsecurityintelligence.com/social-security-survivor-benefits-and-death

---

3   https://oig.ssa.gov/newsroom/blog/may3-widow-underpayments

CHAPTER TAKEAWAYS:

- The survivors benefit can be up to 100% of the benefit of the deceased.

- The widow's limit is up to 82.5% of the deceased spouse's full retirement age benefit.

- Surviving spouses can still use filing strategies that are not available to others.

Chapter 6

Paying Taxes on Social Security

Paying income taxes on Social Security benefits can be a big shock. I clearly remember it was one of my Dad's biggest retirement surprises. Like a lot of other retirees, he didn't know that up to 85% of his Social Security benefit could be counted as taxable income. Ultimately, we were able to mitigate some of his tax burden, but he still owed on other parts of the income. My Dad didn't like that one bit, and he's not alone.

Every year, individuals retire and are faced with sticker shock when they find out how much they'll have to pay in taxes on Social Security income. To some, it doesn't seem fair. You've worked for years and paid your Social Security tax as the admission ticket to a Social Security benefit. Now that you're collecting that benefit, you have to pay taxes? Again?

It wasn't always this way, but it all changed with the passage of 1983 Amendments to the Social Security Act.[4] Under this new rule, up to 50% of Social Security benefits were taxable

---

4   https://www.ssa.gov/history/1983amend.html

for certain individuals. 10 years later, the Deficit Reduction Act of 1993 expanded the taxation of Social Security benefits. Under this act, an additional bracket was added, in which up to 85% of Social Security benefits could be taxable above certain thresholds.

The combination of these laws left us with the current tax structure on Social Security benefits. Today, somewhere between 0% and 85% of your Social Security payment will be included as taxable income.[5] Your Social Security benefit will never be 100% taxable. The maximum amount of benefits that can be included as income is 85%.

To determine how much of your Social Security benefits will be taxable, you first must calculate "provisional income" – a measurement of income used specifically for this purpose. Provisional income can be roughly calculated as your total income from taxable sources, plus any tax-exempt interest (such as interest from tax free bonds), plus any excluded foreign income, plus 50% of your Social Security benefits.

PROVISIONAL INCOME

Adjusted gross income

+ Tax Exempt Income

+ Excluded Foreign Income

+ 50% of Social Security Benefit

= Provisional Income

---

5   https://www.ssa.gov/planners/taxes.html

Once you've calculated your "provisional income" you can apply it to the threshold tables to determine what percentage of your Social Security will be included as taxable income. If your total "provisional income" is less than $32,000 ($25,000 if single), none of your Social Security benefits will be taxable. However, once your total exceeds $32,000 ($25,000 for singles), then part of your benefits become taxable as income.

PROVISIONAL INCOME		
SINGLE	MARRIED FILING JOINTLY	% OF BENEFITS ARE TAXABLE
$0-$25k	$0-$32k	0%
$25k-$34k	$32k-$44k	50%
Above $34k	Above $44k	85%

CHAPTER TAKEAWAYS:

- Up to 85% of your Social Security benefits may be taxable.

- The "provisional income" calculation only includes 50% of your Social Security benefit but 100% of your other income.

PART II

THE SPECIFIC SOCIAL SECURITY RULES FOR TEACHERS AND EDUCATORS

Chapter 7
Special Rules Just for Public Servants

Now that you have a better overview of the Social Security basics, it's time to dig into the additional rules that only apply to certain workers. The most common group of impacted professionals are teachers. However, in many locations, this could also apply to individuals who worked as firefighters, police officers, and numerous other state, county and local employees.

In short, these rules pertain to workers who:

1. Had a job where they did not pay Social Security taxes, *and*

2. Qualified for a pension from that job.

If an individual meets *both* criteria, their Social Security benefits may be subject to two Social Security rules known as the Windfall Elimination Provision and the Government Pension Offset.

- The **Windfall Elimination Provision (WEP)** is a reduction to *your own Social Security benefit* amount from work that you have done.

- The **Government Pension Offset (GPO)** is a reduction to *Social Security spousal or survivors benefits* to which you are entitled based on the work record of another individual, such as a spouse.

Windfall Elimination Provision (WEP)	Government Pension Offset (GPO)
Affects your own Social Security benefit you have earned from work where you paid into Social Security	Affects the benefits you are entitled to as an eligible spouse or survivor of someone who earned a Social Security Benefit

Since these rules are often confused with each other, we'll break each of these down into their own chapters. But first, why do these rules even exist?

Why Do These Rules Exist?

Today, 96% of all workers are covered by Social Security according to the U.S. Government Accountability Office. This has not always been the case. When Social Security was first introduced, the program completely excluded state and local government employees from coverage because there was some doubt as to whether or not the federal government had the right to tax state and local government workers. So, only employees of private companies were allowed to participate.

With the Social Security amendments in the 1950s, state and local employees were given the opportunity to elect to participate in the Social Security system.[6] This decision wasn't left up to the individual employees though. Each state had to enter into an agreement with the Social Security Administration through a "Section 218" agreement. Throughout the 1960s and 1970s most states entered into a Section 218 agreement, but 15 states chose to stay with their own pension plan and not participate in Social Security. These states believed that they could better provide for their retirees with only their pension plan than a combination of their pension plan and Social Security.

The Birth of the Government Pension Offset Rule

Once coverage was available to state and local workers, there were some who took notice of the fact that government workers could retire with a government pension and draw a full spousal or survivors benefit from Social Security. This upset many of them who believed that receiving these benefits at the same time wasn't fair and was a form of "double dipping."

The 1977 Social Security amendments determined that a government pension would have the same treatment as a Social Security benefit. This triggered the "dual entitlement" prohibition that prevents someone from receiving their own Social Security benefit plus a full spousal or survivors

---

6   https://www.brookings.edu/wp-content/uploads/2016/06/
     Download-the-paper-5.pdf

benefit.[7] That's how the Government Pension Offset rule came into effect.

The Birth of the Windfall Elimination Provision

A few years later, in 1983, the Windfall Elimination Provision was signed into law[8]. Like the Government Pension Offset, this new law was meant to insure the fair treatment of everyone with regard to Social Security benefits. However, this Windfall Elimination Provision rule was aimed directly at individuals who qualified for a Social Security benefit from their own work, either before or after working at a job where they did not pay Social Security tax.

The thinking behind this rule was that Social Security benefits were intended as a safety net. The formula for benefits are meant to deliver a "replacement rate" of pre-retirement earnings. The entire system is progressive in that it delivers a higher replacement rate for lower income earners and a lower replacement rate for higher income earners -- because, presumably, those who earned less need more of a safety net and those who earned more do not.

This appeared as a "windfall" for those with non-covered earnings because in the benefit formula, these years would be calculated the same as years with no earnings. This effectively made an individual with both non-covered and covered earnings appear as if they were low-income workers and therefore, they could receive a larger percentage of pre-

7   https://www.ssa.gov/policy/docs/ssb/v41n3/v41n3p3.pdf
8   https://www.ssa.gov/history/1983amend.html

retirement earnings than someone with their total lifetime earnings *should* have received.

The fix? Change the formula to produce a lower benefit for anyone who worked both at a job with covered and non-covered earnings.

While both of these rules were made with the intent of fairness to everyone, the result often does the opposite. With only 4% of the working population covered by these complex rules, there aren't many sources of knowledge and information. This deficit of knowledge about this subject area has led many individuals to make decisions about their retirement that are based in misinformation and bad advice.

I think that everyone should have the ability to clearly plan their future and understand how the various factors will impact them in retirement. That's the goal of this book, and the rest of Part II should provide the information you need to make *good* decisions about planning for your retirement needs.

CHAPTER TAKEAWAYS:

- These special rules only apply if you have qualified for a pension from work where you did not pay Social Security taxes.

- These rules were put into place because drawing both Social Security and a teachers pension was viewed as double dipping.

Chapter 8
The Windfall Elimination Provision

If you only worked in jobs that did not require you to pay Social Security taxes, the Windfall Elimination Provision does not apply to you since you're not eligible for Social Security benefits from your own work. However, if you have employment where you did not pay Social Security taxes, *and also* employment where you *did* pay Social Security taxes (or mixed employment) it becomes hard to calculate your actual Social Security benefit.

How do you know what to expect if you qualify for both Social Security and a public pension? Don't expect it to be on your Social Security statement! Any reduction in benefits thanks to your public servants retirement pension is *not* reflected in the benefits estimate section of your statement. Why? The Social Security Administration does not know about your eligibility status of a pension from non-covered work. They'll only find this out during the process of you applying for benefits.

If you expect to receive a pension from work where you did not pay Social Security taxes, you should understand that your Social Security benefits estimate is wrong -- possibly by several hundred dollars per month. But if you know the rules on the WEP, it doesn't take long to calculate what your benefits will be.

The WEP is simply a recalculation of your Social Security benefit if you also have a pension from "non-covered" work, which is work from which no Social Security taxes are paid. The normal Social Security calculation formula is substituted with a new calculation that results in a lower Social Security benefit amount.

The WEP Guarantee

Just to complicated matters a little more, there is a provision called the WEP Guarantee. The WEP Guarantee is designed to limit the amount that the WEP will reduce your Social Security benefits. Under the WEP Guarantee, your Social Security benefit cannot be reduced by more than half the amount of your non-covered pension, regardless of the WEP calculation amounts. For example, if your non-covered pension amount was $600, the WEP could never reduce your Social Security benefits by more than $300.

Even better, there is a cap on the monthly reduction. For those filing at full retirement age, this reduction is capped at a monthly reduction of $448 (for 2018).[9]

---

9   https://www.ssa.gov/planners/retire/wep-chart.html

The Danger of Relying on Your Social Security Statement

To show just how wrong your Social Security statement can be when estimating benefits but *not* accounting for WEP, take the story of Janice as a cautionary tale. Janice worked as an engineer for 11 years before switching careers to education. She was a detailed planner and had a carefully thought-out retirement plan from an early age. She set a monthly retirement spending goal and subtracted the amount she would receive from her teacher's retirement and Social Security. The amount left would have to be made up with savings.

For the next 20 years, she diligently worked her retirement plan. A few years before retirement, she came to me for a second opinion of her plan. Everything looked great until I saw what she was estimating from her Social Security. All her calculations were based upon the incorrect amount of Social Security income. Her actual benefit would be about $400 *lower* per month. The worst part is that she had taken her estimate directly from her Social Security statement!

Janice's mistake was easy to make, and common. As part of her annual retirement plan update, she would go to her Social Security Administration account and check her benefit estimate. Since she was no longer contributing to Social Security, she knew that the only increases would be from the cost of living adjustment. But Janice, like most others, missed the language on page two of the statement:

"In the future, if you receive a pension from employment in which you do not pay Social Security taxes, such as some

federal, state or local government work, some nonprofit organizations or foreign employment, and you also qualify for your own Social Security retirement or disability benefit, your Social Security benefit may be reduced, but not eliminated, by WEP. The amount of the reduction, if any, depends on your earnings and number of years in jobs in which you paid Social Security taxes, and the year you are age 62 or become disabled."

Thankfully, there is a way to estimate what your benefit will be *after* the reduction for the Windfall Elimination Provision.

How To Calculate Your Real Benefit

The WEP Calculator is one of the best-kept secrets on the 110,000 page Social Security website. You can find it, along with 10 other calculators, on their calculators page located at https://www.ssa.gov/planners/benefitcalculators.html. You put in a few pieces of information, and receive an accurate estimate of your Social Security benefits *after* the WEP reduction is factored in. Here's the step-by-step guide to using the calculator:

STEP 1: Get Your Earnings History

If you don't have a recent Social Security statement handy, here's a quick guide to accessing yours on the Social Security Administration website: https://socialsecurityintelligence. com/social-security-earnings-record/

STEP 2: Go to the Calculator

The easiest way to get there is to visit the page directly. The URL is https://www.ssa.gov/planners/retire/anyPiaWepjs04. html. However, if you want to see the other calculators that are available, you can go to the main benefit calculators page with the URL listed in the introduction of this section.

STEP 3: Enter Information

This calculator does not require you to enter several pages of data to get your calculation results. The only thing you need is your date of birth, proposed age at retirement, earnings information (historical and future) and pension amount. We'll go through each step to make sure it makes sense.

The "Date of Birth" section is self-explanatory. However, the "Age at Retirement" is important. This should be the age at which you plan to file for Social Security benefits, which is not necessarily the age at which you plan to stop working. The Social Security Administration loves to assume that you will file for benefits at the same time you stop working. For an individual with a well thought-out retirement plan, that is not always the case.

Your estimated future benefit amount can be expressed in "today's dollars" or "future dollars." If you select "today's dollars" you will not have any increases applied to your benefit amount to account for inflation. If you select "future dollars," the calculator will increase your benefit by a designated amount every year.

When selecting the inflation option, I strongly suggest using the "today's dollars" option. If you use the "future dollars" option, it will assume your benefit will increase by 2.6% per year from now until you file for benefits That's simply too high! I suggest using "today's dollars."

Non-covered pension amount Enter the monthly amount of your non-covered pension. This is for a Windfall Elimination Provision (WEP) calculation, which should be used only by people who have pensions from work not covered by Social Security. If you do not have a non-covered pension, you should use the Online Calculator, because the WEP calculation could be incorrect.

0

You can estimate the amount of your pension from your non-covered work. In most cases, your pension paying agency can help you estimate the correct amount based on a few projections. The reason this is important for this calculation is due to the WEP Guarantee rule that we touched on above. Remember, the guarantee states that your reduction to Social Security benefits from the WEP can never be greater than an amount equal to one-half of your pension. So, if your pension is $600, the WEP reduction can never be more than $300. This rule only affects a small number of individuals since the maximum reduction that can be applied is $428 (for 2017) no matter how much your pension is.

Annual earnings	Enter your annual earnings from 1951 to 2016.		
Notice that years in the chart are shown horizontally rather than vertically. You can tab from year to year and the zeros will be overlaid.	Note: if you were born after 1951, any earnings you enter before your year of birth will be ignored.		
1951 earnings: 0	1952: 0	1953: 0	
1954: 0	1955: 0	1956: 0	
1957: 0	1958: 0	1959: 0	
1960: 0	1961: 0	1962: 0	
1963: 0	1964: 0	1965: 0	
1966: 0	1967: 0	1968: 0	
1969: 0	1970: 0	1971: 0	
1972: 0	1973: 0	1974: 0	
1975: 0	1976: 0	1977: 0	
1978: 0	1979: 0	1980: 0	
1981: 0	1982: 0	1983: 0	
1984: 0	1985: 0	1986: 0	
1987: 0	1988: 0	1989: 0	
1990: 0	1991: 0	1992: 0	
1993: 0	1994: 0	1995: 0	
1996: 0	1997: 0	1998: 0	
1999: 0	2000: 0	2001: 0	
2002: 0	2003: 0	2004: 0	
2005: 0	2006: 0	2007: 0	
2008: 0	2009: 0	2010: 0	
2011: 0	2012: 0	2013: 0	
2014: 0	2015: 0	2016: 0	

Now, you can just put in your historical annual earnings information from your Social Security statement. You should only plug in earnings that you are going to pay Social Security tax on. If you are not going to pay Social Security taxes, leave a zero in both boxes.

Earnings in 2017

Enter the amount you expect to earn in 2017.
0

Earnings in 2018 and later

Enter the amount you expect to earn in 2018. The calculator will use this same amount of earnings for each future year up to the year you expect to stop working.
0

This is the section that allows you to test how different scenarios will affect your Social Security benefit. For example, if you are considering a job leaving your non-covered job and taking a job that pays into Social Security, you can put the future earnings in to measure your Social Security benefit increase versus your potential decrease in pension payments.

The one downside to this calculator is that it doesn't allow you to input variable earnings for future years. If you want to do that, you'll need to download the detailed calculator located at https://www.ssa.gov/OACT/anypia/anypia.html. Fair warning though: the detailed calculator is a lot more complicated to use than the online calculators. You'll have to refer to the Social Security Administration's help section to understand the steps.

STEP 4: Calculate

Woo hoo! That glorious moment has arrived. It's time to hit the 'Calculate Benefit' button and check your results.

STEP 5: Interpret Results

Now that you've calculated the results, you'll see two main sections. The first section will list your eligibility for the various benefits and the second section will list the projection of the dollar value of your benefits.

Benefit eligibility

You must have sufficient earnings over a number of years to be insured for benefits. The requirements vary for retirement, disability, and survivor benefits. With the information you provided, these are the benefits you are eligible for:

Retirement insured status:

Disability insured status:

Survivor insured status:

The "benefit eligibility" shouldn't cause any confusion. It will say either "Insured" or "Not Insured" in each of the different benefit boxes. This simply means that you have, or have not, earned enough credits for coverage in under each of the categories of benefits. What yours will say is dependent on your work history and if you've earned enough Social Security credits in each of the benefit types. All three of these benefit types have different entitlement requirements.

Benefit estimates

Here are your benefit estimates.

Your monthly retirement benefit:

For the disability and survivors estimates that follow, we assumed you will become disabled or die in 2017. We did not use earnings after 2017 in calculating these estimates.

Your monthly disability benefit:

Your monthly survivor benefits:

Your surviving child:

Your surviving spouse caring for your child:

Your surviving spouse at full retirement age:

Maximum of total family benefits:

Under the benefits estimates section you'll see a few different benefit amounts listed:

- *Monthly retirement benefit*: This is simply the amount of benefit you'll be entitled to at the age you indicated in the "age at retirement" section.

- *Monthly disability benefit*: This should be really close to your full retirement age benefit amount and is the amount you should receive if you become disabled before you retire.

- *Your surviving child*: If you die, your surviving children are eligible for a benefit of up to 75% of your full retirement age benefit.

- *Your surviving spouse caring for your child*: If you die and have children of a certain age at home, your spouse is entitled to a benefit equal to 100% of your full retirement age benefit. This is known as the child-in-care benefit.

- *Your surviving spouse at full retirement age*: Your surviving spouse will be eligible for 100% of your full retirement age benefit at his/her full retirement age. However, they can file as early as age 60 and receive reduced benefits.

- *Maximum of total family benefits*: In no case will the total amount of benefits paid exceed 180% of your full retirement age benefit. In fact, the range is 150-180% depending on your retirement benefit.

If you have a pension from a job that does not contribute to the Social Security program, you'll see that this calculator gives you different results from the simple estimation of benefits available from Social Security. This amount may be tiny, or it could be substantial -- but it is important either way. Correct information, which you can obtain by going through the steps listed above, will give you the right math for your retirement planning. As a result, you can make better financial decisions overall that may result in a better quality of life once you stop working and rely on your nest egg -- and benefits -- to fund your lifestyle.

CHAPTER TAKEAWAYS:

- The reduction from the Windfall Elimination provision is not reflected in your Social Security statement.

- There is a monthly cap on the amount of reduction that can be applied.

- The WEP can never be larger than one half of your pension amount.

- Getting an accurate Social Security benefit requires using a calculator since the Social Security statement does not reflect the reduction.

Chapter 9

The WEP, When You File, and How It Impacts Family Benefits

So, what happens if you file early? Your benefit amount is reduced due to your age, but does the WEP penalty decrease as well? The same question could be asked about if you wait until beyond your full retirement age to file. Will your penalty amount increase? The Social Security Administration has a page where they discuss this, but it is not clearly or concisely written (which will be no surprise if you've ever tried to make sense of the SSA site before).[10]

The WEP Effect on Filing Early or Late

The WEP reduces your benefit amount *before* it is reduced or increased due to early retirement or delayed retirement credits. It is this WEP-reduced benefit that is increased, or decreased, due to filing age.

For example, let's assume Sue is 66 and has a Social Security benefit of $1,448. The "maximum" WEP penalty that could

---

10   https://www.ssa.gov/planners/retire/wep-examples.html

be applied is $448. This gives her a WEP reduced benefit of $1,000 ($1,448 − $448 = $1,000). If Sue files for her benefits at 66, her benefit is $1,000 after the reduction for WEP. In this case, the WEP penalty amount is exactly $448. If Sue files for benefit at 62, she would receive a reduced benefit since she is filing early.

Remember, her benefit will be reduced for the WEP first and then reduced based on her filing age. This is how it looks in the calculation:

$1,428 Full Retirement Age Benefit
- $448 WEP Penalty
$1,000 benefit after reduction for WEP
- $250 reduction for filing age ($1,000 − 25%)
$750 benefit after reduction for WEP and filing age

If Sue were not subject to the WEP, and still filed at 62, her benefit would be $1,071. However, since she is subject to the penalty, her total benefit is $750. This means the effective penalty is $321. The same is true if Sue delays filing.

If Sue were *not* subject to the WEP, and filed for benefits at 70, her benefit would be $1,885 due to the delayed retirement credits discussed in Part I of this book:

$1,428 Full Retirement Age Benefit
- $448 WEP Penalty
$1,000 benefit after reduction for WEP
+ $320 increase for filing age ($1,000 + 32%)
$1,320 benefit after reduction for WEP and increase for filing age

$1,885 – Filing at 70 without WEP
$1,320 – Filing at 70 with WEP
  $565   Effective Penalty

The Effect of the WEP to Family Benefits

Social Security benefits aren't just for you They can also be paid to eligible spouses and children. However, the benefit upon which those payments are based will also be reduced under the WEP.

First, let's take a quick refresher in the benefits available for your family. There are benefits available to your children and spouse if you die, become disabled or retire. Refer to the chart below see what percentage is available under each qualifying condition, age restrictions and whether or not the earnings limit is applied:

	% of YOUR Full Retirement Age Benefit Amount Family Members Are Potentially Entitled To If You:			
	Die	Retire (or) Become Disabled	Age Restrictions	Subject to Earning's Limit?
Spouse Benefit	100% (will be reduced if surviving spouse files prior to his/her full retirement age)	50% (will be reduced if surviving spouse files prior to his/her full retirement age)	DIE - Surviving spouse can file at 60 (50 if he/she is disabled) BECOME DISABLED - Spouse can file at 62	Yes - Until surviving spouse's Full Retirement Age
Child in Care Spousal Benefit	100%	50%	Until child is 16	Yes
Benefit to Children	75%	50%	Until child is 18 (or 19 if still in high school or) No age restriction if child has a disability that began prior to age 22	Yes - Parent's earnings do not count. Only child's earnings.
	Total Benefits Paid Are Limited By The Family Benefit Maximum			

For example, imagine that your non-WEP reduced full retirement age benefit is $1,000. After the reduction, it would be $552. It's this amount that will be used to calculate benefits payable to your spouse and children.

If you have a spouse who has never worked, they would still be eligible for a spousal benefit. However, that spousal benefit would be reduced because it is based on your benefit amount.

No WEP Reduction

$1,000 - Your full retirement age benefit
$500 - Max Spousal benefit
$1,500 - Total family benefit

With WEP Reduction

$552 - Your full retirement age benefit
$276 - Max Spousal benefit
$828 - Total family benefit

In this example, the penalty amount that is applied against the total amount of benefits is a whopping $672!

It's important to note that if you die, your Social Security benefit will be recalculated with the normal formula and the WEP penalty will no longer apply. In that case, your eligible spouse and children would have their benefit based on the $1,000 instead of the reduced $552.

CHAPTER TAKEAWAYS:

- The reduction from the Windfall Elimination Provision is not reflected in your Social Security statement.

- The WEP penalty is subtracted from your benefit amount before it is reduced or increased due to early retirement or delayed retirement credits.

- If you are subject to the WEP, any benefits paid to others which are based on your benefit amount are also reduced.

Chapter 10

Two Ways to Get Around the WEP

Feeling like you're stuck with this tricky provision? There may be a way out. In fact, there are two official ways around the WEP. You need to understand both so you can take advantage if it works for you and your situation.

The WEP Offset Phase-Out

If you have mixed earnings, and you paid into the Social Security system for more than 20 years, there is a phase-out of the WEP offset. This requires that these earnings be "substantial," as defined by the Social Security administration and listed in a chart on their website.[11] Workers with 21 to 29 years of substantial covered earnings are eligible for a partial exemption from the WEP. At 30 years of substantial covered earnings, the WEP does not apply.

---

11 https://www.ssa.gov/pubs/EN-05-10045.pdf

Years of Substantial Earnings	Maximum WEP Reduction (2018)
20 or less	$448
21	$403
22	$358
23	$314
24	$269
25	$224
26	$179
27	$134
28	$90
29	$45
30	$0

This phase-out of the WEP reduction offers an incredible planning opportunity if you have worked at a job where you paid Social Security tax.[12] For example, if you worked as an engineer for 20 years before you began teaching, you may be able to do enough part-time work between now and when you retire to completely eliminate the monthly WEP reduction. Or, if your spouse is self employed, it could make sense to put yourself on payroll for the purposes of accumulating these years of substantial earnings.

Would it be worth it? If you consider how much more in benefits you could receive over your retirement lifetime, it could be worth $100,000 in extra income over a 20-year retirement. Obviously, not everyone has the option of accumulating enough years to wipe out the big monthly WEP reduction. But for those who do, or can get close, it's worth taking a closer look.

It's important to note that the years of substantial service do not have to be met when you file for benefits. If at any time you accumulate enough years, you can request for

---

12   https://www.socialsecurity.gov/planners/retire/wep-chart.html

your benefit to be recalculated to reflect the lower penalty. If you want to use this loophole, you need to check your earnings history and mark the years that meet the definition of "substantial." And don't hesitate to question the accuracy of your earnings record! As discussed in chapter 1, earnings records mistakes are not uncommon. For someone trying to meet the definition of "substantial" earnings, it is even more crucial to check your earnings history!

The Lump Sum Pension Withdrawal

Often, individuals will wonder if they can sidestep these rules by simply taking their pension in a lump sum. After all, in just about every reference to these rules, the Social Security Administration says that the rules apply to individuals with a pension from work where no Social Security taxes were paid.

It makes sense to wonder: if there's no "pension," do the rules still apply?

They do, but with a few exceptions. For certain individuals, taking a pension out in a lump sum can be a valid method of sidestepping these rules. Not all pension plans allow withdrawals of lump sums, but there are some who do allow either partial lump sum withdrawals or allow you to withdraw everything in the plan.

In most cases, if you take a withdrawal from this non-covered pension, the Social Security Administration will use an alternate calculation to determine the amount you would have received based on your age and the date you took the lump sum. Even though you take it in a lump sum, it'll be viewed as if you took a normal pension.

The Social Security website has this to say about the issue:

"When the entire pension is paid in a lump sum, the amount may represent a payment for a specific period of time or a "lifetime." Generally, the pension-paying agency will prorate the lump sum to determine a monthly amount for WEP purposes. If the agency will not provide this information, prorate the lump sum to determine the monthly pension amount as follows:

Specific Period - Divide the lump sum by the number of months in the period specified by the pension-paying agency. See RS 00605.360C.5.a. for when WEP application ends.

Lifetime or Unspecified Period - Divide the pension lump sum amount by the appropriate actuarial value in the table that corresponds to the worker's age on the date of the lump sum award."

This language does two things: It directs the Social Security technician how to treat your lump sum pension, and it also directs the Social Security Administration as to when the WEP should no longer affect your benefit payment. It's important to note that if you receive a payment in lieu of a pension for a certain period, the end of that period is when the WEP application will end.

For example, if your lump sum payment was made in lieu of a 10-year payment period, the WEP would no longer affect you after 10 years. If no period is selected, the Social Security technician will use a table on their website to determine how long the payments should have lasted. At the end of that period, the WEP would no longer be applied. So, even if your plan will allow you to do a full or partial withdrawal of your pension, that alone will not help you get around the rules.

The only way to sidestep the rules is to take out only your contributions plus interest. Even then, the timing must be just right and there are separate rules for getting around the Windfall Elimination Provision and the Government Pension Offset. To sidestep the WEP, you must take out your contributions *before you become eligible* for a pension. Once you've reached eligibility, it's too late to withdraw your contributions and avoid the Windfall Elimination Provision.

Here's what the Social Security website says in their section RS 00605.364 Determining Pension Applicability, Eligibility Date, and Monthly Amount:

"Withdrawals of the employee's own contributions and interest made before the employee is eligible to receive a pension are not pensions for WEP purposes if the employee forfeits all rights to the pension. This rule applies even if the employer paid the employee contributions.

Withdrawals of the employee's own contributions and interest made after the employee is eligible to receive a pension are considered a lump-sum pension for WEP purposes.

Any separation payment, withdrawal, or refund consisting of both employer and employee contributions is a pension; for WEP purposes whether made before or after the employee is eligible to receive a pension."

It's crucial to understand the meaning of the word *eligibility* as defined by the Social Security Administration. It does not mean that you have stopped work! In fact, you could still be working and deemed "eligible" for your pension. This is disastrous to those individuals who planned to wait until a week before they retired to withdraw their contributions. In another section of the Social Security website, they define "eligibility" as follows:

"An individual becomes eligible for a monthly pension or a lump sum in lieu of a monthly pension the first month he or she meets all requirements for payment except stopping work and applying for the payment [emphasis added]."

So, could you still be working and technically eligible for your pension? Yes! If you plan to withdraw your contributions to avoid the WEP, you'll need to know exactly what it takes to become "eligible" for a pension at your employer. For example, if you are working in Texas, you'll become eligible for a pension at age 55 with 5 or more years of service credit. If you are planning to stop working at 56, and wait until then to withdraw your pension, it'll be too late.

In all but a few isolated cases, a complete withdrawal from your pension plan to escape the WEP penalty just doesn't make sense. You have to leave all of the employer contributions behind and forgo your rights to the pension checks. Sure, you'll get penalty free Social Security benefits, but the amount of additional benefits is usually much smaller than the pension you left behind.

CHAPTER TAKEAWAYS:

- The amount of the WEP penalty is lowered if you have between 20 and 30 years which meet the definition of substantial earnings.

- Taking a non-covered pension in a lump sum will still trigger the WEP.

Chapter 11

The Nuts and Bolts of the WEP Calculation

In Part I, we discussed the basics of how Social Security benefits are calculated. Let's revisit the "normal" formula and then see how the benefit formula is different for those with a non-covered pension.

When Social Security benefits are calculated, the SSA inflates all of your historical earrings which were subject to Social Security taxes, extracts your highest 35 years of earnings, and divides by 420 (the number of months in 35 years). This gives the inflation-adjusted average indexed monthly earnings, or your AIME. Your AIME is then applied to the formula and the result is your primary insurance amount (PIA). This is also known as your full retirement age benefit.

Normal Social Security Formula (2018)		
Indexed Earnings	Multiplier	Social Security Benefit at Full Retirement Age
$0-$896	90%	
$897-$5,399	32%	
$5,400 +	15%	

If you have a pension from work where no Social Security was paid, your benefits are calculated on an alternate formula. The result of this alternate formula is a lower benefit amount. At first glance this alternate formula looks nearly identical to the 'normal' formula. However, upon closer inspection you'll notice that the earnings between $0 and $896 are credited to your final Social Security benefit at 40% instead of the 90% found in the normal formula.

WEP Social Security Formula (2018)		
Indexed Earnings	Multiplier	Social Security Benefit at Full Retirement Age
$0-$896	40%	
$897-$5,399	32%	
$5,400 +	15%	

The difference between the result of the 'normal' calculation and the WEP calculation is where the penalty amount comes from. This is also where the "years of substantial service" begin to reduce your penalty amount. Remember that if you have 20 years or less of substantial earnings, the full penalty applies. This means that the 90% multiplier is replaced with the 40% multiplier. Between 21 and 30 years of substantial earnings the percentage increases by 5% for every year of substantial earnings. At 30 years, the multiplier is back to 90%.

Years of substantial earnings	Percentage
30 or more	90%
29	85%
28	80%
27	75%
26	70%
25	65%
24	60%
23	55%
22	50%
21	45%
20 or less	40%

CHAPTER TAKEAWAYS:

- The WEP is simply an alternate calculation of your Social Security benefit.

- The top multiplier in the formula changes for every year of substantial earnings between 21 through 30.

Chapter 12

The Government Pension Offset

The other penalty that applies to individuals with non-covered pensions is called the Government Pension Offset (GPO). The GPO is a reduction to Social Security survivor or spouse benefits for those who are receiving a pension from their own work that was not covered under the Social Security system.

The mechanics of the Government Pension Offset are simple. If you have a pension from non-covered employment (no Social Security tax paid), the Social Security benefits you receive as a spouse or survivor will be reduced by an amount equal to two-thirds of your *gross* pension.

I've had more than one client who was shocked to find they wouldn't receive a spousal or survivor's benefit due to the GPO. It can seem incredibly unfair and can come as a nasty surprise -- especially if you've been planning your retirement income with this stream of payments calculated in.

When (and to Whom) the GPO Applies

An important note is that the GPO can only be applied to the individual who earned the non-covered pension. One of the questions I often receive is, "If I leave my pension payments to my spouse, will that affect their Social Security?"

I understand why there is confusion on this. After all, the Social Security rules continuously discuss that the GPO applies if you are receiving a pension from non-covered work. It makes sense that if your spouse leaves you as a beneficiary on their pension from non-covered work, the same penalties may apply to them. The SSA answers this succinctly in their rule book, saying, "the Government Pension Offset (GPO) applies to a spouse's Social Security benefit for any month the spouse receives a pension **based upon his or her own government employment not covered under Social Security."** The emphasis is theirs.

The short answer is that their Social Security benefits *would not* be affected if you left them as a beneficiary on your pension.

How to Calculate How GPO Impacts Your Benefits

To figure out how much your benefits will be reduced by the GPO, you first must figure out your regular spousal or survivors benefits (see Part I for more information on this). Then, take the gross amount of your pension from non-covered employment, and subtract it from the amount of spousal or survivors benefits calculated using the regular formula.

Let's consider the case of Ann as an example. Ann worked as a schoolteacher for 30 years and her husband was an accountant. Her teaching years were spent in Texas, one of the 15 states where teachers are not covered by Social Security. When she retired, she began receiving her Texas Teachers' Retirement pension of $3,000 per month. Her husband also retired and filed for his Social Security benefits of $2,200 per month. Sadly, her husband passed away two years later.

She was devastated by his passing -- and it didn't help to find out that she would not continue to receive his full Social Security benefit. Instead, the Government Pension Offset kicked in and reduced her survivor's benefit down to a measly $200 per month:

GPO Reduction Formula	
$3,000	Ann's Pension
x 2/3	
$2,000	Reduction to Social Security Survivor's or Spousal Benefits
GPO Reduction Applied	
$2,200	Ann's Social Security Survivor Benefit
(-)$2,000	GPO Reduction
$200	Ann's Social Security Survivor Benefit After GPO Reduction

The GPO only applies because of Ann's chosen profession and the choice by her employer not to work with Social Security. This is effectively a penalty for public service -- and that fact is where the title of this book comes from! If Anne worked as an accountant instead, she would have been eligible to receive the full $2,200 per month. Thankfully, there is a way to get around the GPO, and we'll discuss that in the coming chapters.

CHAPTER TAKEAWAYS:

- The GPO will reduce Social Security Spousal or survivors benefits by an amount equal to ⅔ of your pension.

- The GPO can completely eliminate your Social Security Spousal or survivors benefits.

Chapter 13
Getting Around the GPO

If you want to sidestep the effect of the GPO and collect a full Social Security spousal or survivors benefit, there are two ways to do so. Both of these workarounds could require some pretty drastic moves, but depending on your situation, one of these options may make sense for you.

GPO Workaround Option 1: The Last 60 Month Rule

The first way to get around the GPO is called the Last 60 Month Rule.[13] Here's how it works: You need to work at a job where you contribute to *both* Social Security and the same non-covered pension as your previous job for the last 60 months of employment.

In other words, this means you must leave your job and find new employment that is covered by the same retirement plan as your old job, but is also covered by Social Security. It may not be possible, but it's an option if you can find a position that checks both these boxes like Dave did.

---

13   https://secure.ssa.gov/poms.nsf/lnx/0202608107

Dave worked for Lancaster TX Independent School District (ISD) for 30 years. Since Lancaster only participated in Texas Teachers' Retirement system (TRS), but not Social Security, Dave would normally have faced the Government Pension Offset when he retired. But Dave quit Lancaster and spent the last 60 months of his career working for Austin ISD, a school district that participated in both Social Security and Texas TRS. By doing so, he exempted himself from the provisions of the GPO.

How far-fetched is this? Depending on your state, there may be a decent list of community colleges or school districts that participate in both Social Security and your state teachers' retirement pension. But would it be worth the hassle of a late-career change to exempt yourself from the GPO? Here are some numbers to help you decide for yourself:

Let's assume that your spouse has a Social Security benefit of $2,000 per month at their full retirement age. If you can sidestep the GPO, you would be eligible for a spousal benefit of $1,000 per month at your full retirement age. Carrying that out over a 20 year retirement, and adding in a 2% annual cost of living adjustment to the Social Security benefit, leaves you with $291,568 in spousal benefits. If your spouse dies, you'd be eligible for a survivors benefit. Using the same cost of living and life expectancy number, that would be worth $583,136 in lifetime benefit payments.

Potential Value of Workaround	
$291,568	Lifetime Spousal Benefit Payments
$583,136	Lifetime Survivor Benefit Payments
2% Annual Increase Over 20 Years	

There is a really important stipulation to this workaround. If you are trying to get around the GPO by using the last 60 month rule, you should be very careful not mix employment! The Social Security Administration states the following:

"If, at any time during the last 60 months of government service, the individual worked in noncovered employment under the retirement system that provides the pension, the individual's spousal benefit will be subject to GPO. GPO will apply, with regard to that pension, even if the individual concurrently worked in another position with the same or a different employer covered by Social Security. "[14]

In other words, during the period you are fulfilling your last 60 months, you cannot work even one day under employment that does not pay Social Security tax and participates in the same retirement plan. If your old employer asks you to work a couple of weeks during the summer…just say no! It'll ruin everything.

GPO Workaround Option 2: Withdrawal from Your Pension

The second option is to completely withdraw from your pension plan. You'd withdraw your contributions and interest, and forfeit your future rights to the pension. This option may not make any sense at all. In fact, it could place you at a tremendous disadvantage. However, it could be a good avenue for certain individuals in certain pension plans. Again…it all depends on your individual circumstances.

---

14   https://secure.ssa.gov/poms.nsf/lnx/0202608107v

Here's what the Social Security Administration says about this:

*Withdrawals from a defined benefit plan, before or after eligibility for the pension, of **only employee contributions plus any interest** (i.e., none of the employer contributions are included in the withdrawal), and whereby the employee forfeits all rights to a pension, are not pensions for GPO purposes. This rule applies even if the employer paid the employee contributions for the employee (i.e., some employers may pay for the employee's contribution). Any other separation payment, withdrawal, or refund that consists of both employer and employee contributions from a defined benefit or defined contribution plan is a pension subject to GPO.*[15]

The takeaway from this option is that you'd better make sure you are receiving *only* the amount you put in plus interest. If any of the employer contribution is included in the withdrawal, you'll still be subject to the GPO. In many cases, it just doesn't make sense to withdraw your pension. Sure, you may receive a full Social Security benefit if you can avoid the WEP and GPO, but you'll also forfeit your rights to the pension income. For this reason, it generally doesn't make sense.

However, there are very isolated cases where this may be appropriate. If you are thinking about this option, be sure you consider your income needs, the amount of your pension vs. the amount of your spousal/survivors benefits, and a host of other factors. A high-caliber financial planner can help you make sense of your options.

---

15   https://secure.ssa.gov/poms.nsf/lnx/0202608400/#3

CHAPTER TAKEAWAYS:

- To satisfy the Last 60 Month rule, you must pay Social Security taxes in a job that is covered under the same retirement plan as the job where you did not pay Social Security taxes.

- During the last 60 month rule, you cannot mix covered and uncovered employment.

- A complete withdrawal from your pension may exempt you from the GPO, but may not make sense because you'll have to forfeit your pension income.

Chapter 14

Mixed Earnings or Mixed Employment

Now that we've covered the essentials of the WEP and GPO, let's dive into a few areas that deal with both of these provisions. The first is how to handle earnings that are "mixed" in that some of the contributions to the pension were from covered earnings and some were from non-covered earnings.

In several states, most school districts do not participate in Social Security. Instead, they have their own pension plan to which they contribute. Some school districts in these states, however, have adopted agreements with the Social Security Administration which allows them to participate in both Social Security *and* their own pension plan.

For example, the school districts in my hometown of Texarkana, Texas, do not participate in Social Security. They only contribute into the Teachers' Retirement System of Texas (TRS). However, scattered around my state are several school districts, such as Austin ISD, that participate in Social Security in addition to Texas TRS.

If an educator spends their entire career at either a district that contributes solely to Social Security, or solely into TRS, or solely into both Social Security and TRS, there isn't usually an issue in calculating what their benefits may be. But if someone worked at both types of school districts, this "mixed" employment makes it more challenging to properly calculate how much to expect in Social Security benefits.

It gets complicated due to the Windfall Elimination Provision (WEP) and the Government Pension Offset (GPO), two provisions that apply to anyone with a pension from work where no Social Security taxes were paid -- as you now well know. The WEP applies to an individual's own Social Security benefit, and the GPO applies to survivor or spousal benefits.

On their own, these provisions can be difficult to fully understand. If you add mixed earnings to the equation, they're often nearly incomprehensible. But...it's important to understand how this should be calculated. If you don't understand this, your Social Security benefit amount may be reduced incorrectly.

Calculating WEP with Mixed Earnings

We'll look at Denise as our example to make sense of all this, and show you how this works in the real world. Denise worked at Austin ISD for 15 years. While in Austin, she paid into Social Security and TRS. When her husband died, she moved to my hometown of Texarkana and started working for Texarkana ISD, where she spent the last 15 years of her teaching career. While in Texarkana, she paid into TRS, but did not pay Social Security taxes.

She retired with a TRS pension of $3,000, and she was also eligible for Social Security benefits. But she wasn't sure how to answer the question of, how much would she receive via those Social Security benefits? She'd always heard about the Social Security provisions that would reduce an educator's benefit amount. But Denise felt confused confused because in her research everything referenced the WEP and GPO applied to individuals with a non-covered pension (a pension where no Social Security taxes were paid). She had a pension and half of it came from work where no Social Security taxes were paid -- but the other half was from her time in Austin where she *did* pay Social Security tax.

She came to me after the Social Security Administration claims representative told her that the work where she paid Social Security taxes didn't matter. But that technician was dead wrong -- and it almost cost Denise several hundred dollars per year in missed benefits.

The Windfall Elimination Provision still applies for those with mixed earnings. But remember the WEP guarantee? Your Social Security benefit can only be reduced by ½ of your non-covered pension. If part of that pension came from covered work, how do you calculate what ½ of the pension is?

Let's say that you worked for 15 years at a covered district and 5 years at a district that is non-covered. If your pension provides you with $2,000 per month, only 25% of it is attributable to the years you spent in the non-covered earnings. Your true "non-covered" pension amount is $500. In this case, the most your WEP penalty could be is half of that amount, or $250.

The WEP is the easier part to figure out when you have mixed employment. Mixed earnings have the most impact on the Government Pension Offset. If you find yourself in this situation, here's how the GPO should be calculated.

Calculating the GPO with Mixed Earnings

The GPO is a reduction to spousal or survivors benefits if you have a pension where you did not pay Social Security taxes. The reduction is 2/3 of your pension amount. For example, if your pension is $3,000, the Social Security Administration will subtract nearly $2,000 from any spousal or survivors benefits before you are paid. This large reduction often completely wipes out any benefit for which you are eligible.

If you have a pension from mixed earnings, the entire pension amount *should not* be used in calculating the 2/3 reduction! You should only use the amount that came from the months where you *did not* pay Social Security taxes.

The Social Security rules make this clear:

"Some entities may pay a pension based on both government employment and private employment. For pensions based on a combination of federal, state, or local government employment and private employment (i.e., non-government employment), GPO applies only to the portion of the pension based on government employment. [emphasis added]."[16]

For example, when Denise filed for benefits they told her that her GPO reduction would be $2,000 (2/3 of her $3,000 pension). Instead, they should have told her that her spousal or survivors benefits would be reduced by *only* $1,000, based

16   https://secure.ssa.gov/poms.nsf/lnx/0202608400

upon the portion of her pension that was earned during years she did not contribute to Social Security. That's a big difference!

What they told her:

> $3,000 - Total Pension
> x   2/3 Reduction
> $2,000 Reduction to spousal or survivors benefits

What they should have told her:

> $1,500 - Prorated pension from noncovered work
> x   2/3 Reduction
> $1,000 Reduction to spousal or survivors benefits

If Denise's monthly survivors benefit should be $2,200 at her full retirement age, the proper calculation of the GPO means that she would still receive $1,200. However, if it was not calculated with the prorated pension, she would only receive $200!

Understanding how this rule works could be an important part of successful retirement planning. For example, someone in Denise's position could file for a survivors benefit only and switch to their own benefit at age 70. This would mean that their own benefit amount would be higher due to the increases for the delayed filing.

How to Prorate Your Pension

The Social Security Administration implies it is simple to verify the amount of your prorated pension, saying you should "request verification from the employer or pension-paying agency showing the amount of the pension based on only the government employment." However, you may run into issues with your pension paying agency giving you this information. Many of them just don't keep these types of records. If that's the case, you'd want to get your employment records, Social Security earnings history, and use the following formula to prorate it yourself:

Pension From Non-Covered Work = Total pension **times** months of non-covered work (post-1956) **divided** by the total months used to calculate pension.

For example, Denise's pension is $3,000. Her months of non-covered work were 180 (15 years). The total months used to calculate pension was 360 (30 years). This calculation would appear as follows: $3,000 x 180 / 360 = $1,500 Amount of pension that is non-covered and thus excluded from the GPO calculations.

For months with both types of earnings, a month that contains both covered and non-covered employment is considered a covered work month.

CHAPTER TAKEAWAYS:

- If your pension is from work that is covered and noncovered, you should be ready to educate the Social Security claims representative on the proper proration procedure.

Chapter 15
403(b) Plans, 457 Accounts, and ORP

Many school districts will offer supplemental retirement plans in addition to their pension plan. Does a distribution from these plans trigger the WEP and GPO? It depends. Let's first examine the 403(b) plans and 457 accounts.

Will Your Plans Trigger WEP or GPO?

Whether or not the amount you've saved there could trigger the WEP and GPO depends on your individual employer. Here's what the Social Security Administration handbook says:

"Payments received from defined contribution plans (e.g., 401(k), 403(b), or 457 plans) based on non-covered employment are considered a pension subject to WEP regardless of the source of contributions (employer only, employee only, or a combination of both), if the plan is the primary retirement plan. If the plan is a supplemental plan, the payments are

subject to WEP when the plan payments contain employer or
both employer and employee contributions."[17]

Essentially, if the 403(b) or 457 is a supplemental plan and
only has your contributions in it, it will not be subject to
the WEP and GPO calculations. If it is your primary plan,
or a supplemental plan with employer contributions, it will
trigger the WEP and GPO calculations. This means that
they will calculate the lump sum amount in your plan as if
you'd taken it in a series of payments like your pension. This
additional amount would be added to your "gross pension
amount" when calculating the ⅔ reduction to spousal or
survivors benefits.

A Special Note for ORP Participants

A book on the complexities of Social Security for educators
wouldn't be complete without a mention of those who work in
higher education -- specifically, those employees of community
colleges and universities who allow you to choose between the
Teacher's Retirement System or an Optional Retirement Plan.
(If this doesn't apply to you, just skip to the next chapter.)

Not too long ago I saw a massive mistake made by a
participant in an Optional Retirement Program. It was a
simple little move that cost her thousands of dollars. To make
matters worse, she made this move on the recommendation
of her financial advisor.

Essentially, certain higher education employees can opt out of
the Teachers Retirement System in favor of a plan that allows
them to make their own contributions and get a match from

---

17   https://secure.ssa.gov/poms.nsf/lnx/0300605364

their employer. The dollars in the plan can be invested in a variety of ways. On the surface it works much like a 401(k) or some other employer sponsored retirement plan. This intent of creating this plan was to give these employees a choice of how they saved for their retirement needs.

The Big Mistake You Could Be Making in the Optional Retirement Plan

The big mistakes that I've seen have not been due to how the funds are invested, but in what happens when the funds begin to be distributed. For those workers who are also eligible for Social Security, there is often a blanket assumption that those benefits will automatically be subject to the reduction from the Windfall Elimination Provision.

That's simply not true. You can get a Social Security benefit that is *not* reduced by the Windfall Elimination Provision into your early 70s *if* you avoid the triggering events. The Social Security Administration has a great piece on Texas ORP and Social Security on their website.[18] (Oddly enough, their website does not specifically mention other states, but in my experience I've found the rules to be very similar.)

The rules found there on how the ORP triggers the WEP can be boiled down to these points:

- The trigger for the WEP reduction does not occur until you become *entitled* to benefits from your ORP.

- Entitlement does not occur until you take a *distribution.*

---

18   https://secure.ssa.gov/poms.nsf/lnx/0300605364DAL

- For purposes of the WEP trigger, a distribution is a rollover of any type, a lump sum distribution, or periodic payments.

- Distributions are required no later than April 1 of the year following the year you attain age 70 ½.

So, as long as you don't meet the triggers, you are not "entitled" to your ORP and thus are not subject to the Windfall Elimination Provision. This could mean several years of a Social Security benefit with *no* reduction. Here's how those rules apply in real life:

Depending on when your birthday falls, on average you have 113 months between age 62 and April 1st of the year *after* you attain age 70 ½. The current maximum WEP reduction is $448 per month. You could file for Social Security benefits at age 62 and have all those months with *no* deduction as long as you don't become "entitled" to your Texas ORP.

That could mean an additional $50,000 in Social Security benefits ($448 per month x 113 months). I should point out that those figures do not include increases from the cost of living adjustment which will make this amount higher.

For some, this may not be an option. You may need the income from these savings dollars right away. However, some strategic retirement income planning may allow you pull income from other sources and eliminate the need for touching those ORP dollars until you are required to take a distribution. And remember that your ORP account can stay where it is when you retire. If your financial advisor tells you that you need to do a rollover (or anything else) with your ORP balances, be *very* inquisitive. There could be $50,000 at stake.

CHAPTER TAKEAWAYS:

- 403(b) plans and 457 accounts will not trigger the WEP & GPO if they are supplemental plans and only include your contributions.

- Distributions from an ORP account should be carefully considered.

Chapter 16

How To Get Social Security Coverage at Your School

Your school district or employer is not locked into an exclusion from Social Security! If you want to change this, and get covered by Social Security, it is possible. If there are enough employees of your school district who believe you should also be covered by Social Security, you can get it changed. Here's why you might want to petition your employer to do so.

If you compare the benefits from most state pensions to Social Security, it becomes obvious that the pension is a usually a better return on investment. Based on the contributions you put in, the retirement income coming out is almost always higher than you can get with the same contributions with Social Security.

Here's the problem: to get this better return you have to work for years in the same retirement plan. Most employees don't stay in one place that long. Sure, if you work for 30 years within the same pension plan, it's a better deal than Social Security. But the reality is, most people don't work that long for one employer and with a state pension. This is unlike Social Security because there's almost no portability. If you leave before you are covered, you'll often simply lose the future pension -- and that's the issue with having *only* a pension.

How to Get Covered

If you want to get Social Security coverage at your employer there is a process to follow. There are several steps but the most important is a vote among the employees. If you want more information on how to get started, and do this correctly, you need to enlist the assistance of your state's Social Security Administrator.

This individual is responsible for all of the Social Security coverage agreements within your state. You can find your administrator at http://ncsssa.org/statessadminmenu.html.

CHAPTER TAKEAWAYS:

- If there are enough employees of your school district who believe you should also be covered by Social Security, you can get it changed.

Chapter 17
Conclusion

As an educator, you've got plenty to keep up with. High stakes testing, difficult parents, students that are not encouraged at home, increasing regulations and teacher turnover that leads to a lack of experienced mentors...

All of these factors can make education a very difficult profession. According to a report by the Robert Wood Johnson Foundation, 46% of teachers report high daily stress levels.[19] This ties them with nurses for the highest rate among all occupational groups. And although I can't help you with the day-to-day stress of educating our future generation, I *can* give you some tips to help with planning for your retirement:

1. Accept that the rules are different for you.

Through the course of reading this book I hope this fact has been well established: you have a different set of rules that apply to you. Accept it and plan around it. Don't hold your breath for Congress to abolish either the WEP or GPO. There have been multiple attempts to do so over the years and none that I know of have even made it out of committee for a floor

---

19   https://www.rwjf.org/content/dam/farm/reports/issue_briefs/2016/rwjf430428

vote. The bills which had the most promise, HR 711, would
have simply replaced the WEP with a new formula and did
nothing for the GPO[20].

This doesn't mean it can't happen, but when something only
affects 4% of the population, as these provisions do, it's hard
to get momentum behind change. I'd accept the fact that you
are not subject to the same rulebook as everyone else and
adapt your plan accordingly.

2. Don't count solely on your pension

According to Pew, there is a $1.4 trillion dollar difference
between the promises states have made to retirees and the
money that's actually set aside to pay these promises. [21] That
doesn't sound like a sound secure promise for tomorrow's
retirement.

While your pension certainly needs to be a part of your
retirement income plan, you absolutely need to supplement
that plan with additional savings in a 403(b), 457 or a
traditional or Roth IRA. Your employer will have more
information on the supplemental plans available to you.

But one warning here! many of the supplemental plans tend
to be offered through insurance companies. If that's the case,
the fees could be excessively high; in some cases they'll be
greater than 2% per year! High fees will rob you of investment
returns. If the only options for retirement savings are with
high-fee providers, consider opening a traditional or Roth
IRA with a low-fee institution.

20   https://www.congress.gov/bill/114th-congress/house-bill/711
21   http://www.pewtrusts.org/en/research-and-analysis/issue-
     briefs/2018/04/the-state-pension-funding-gap-2016

3. Continue what you've started with this book

As an educator, a successful retirement is going to require more planning and self education. These topics are not understood very well by most financial planners and sadly, even the technicians at the Social Security Administration.

This leaves the burden on you. No one will will feel the pain and regret of big retirement mistakes like you will. You can avoid many mistakes by continuing to do what you have done in purchasing this book. Remember, this is your retirement. Take charge!

How to Continue Learning What You Need to Know About Social Security

If you'd like to continue your education in Social Security, here are some additional resources that I'd highly encourage you to use:

- My website at SocialSecurityIntelligence.com
- The videos I have on YouTube[22]
- Big Picture Retirement podcast[23]

Again, I congratulate you for downloading this guide and making it to the conclusion.

You can always find me at SocialSecurityIntelligence.com, where I'll be researching and simplifying the crazy Social Security rules and cheering you on as you navigate the maze of retirement planning and all the complex, nuanced topics that come with it.

---

22   https://www.youtube.com/channel/UCy8uDv16fJTy51bz0iS8T-Q
23   https://www.bigpictureretirement.net/

Made in the USA
Columbia, SC
01 April 2019